HIGH-SPEED TRAINS

FROM CONCEPT TO CONSUMER

BY STEVEN OTFINOSKI

CHILDREN'S PRESS®

An Imprint of Scholastic Inc.

CONTENT CONSULTANT
Drew Galloway, Amtrak

PHOTOGRAPHS ©: cover: Scanrail/Dreamstime; 3: JTB PhotoUIG Universal Images Group/
Newscom; 4 left: Mansell/Getty Images; 4 right: Bloomberg/Getty Images; 5 left: Agencja
Fotograficzna Caro/Alamy Images; 5 right: Media Bakery; 6: Mansell/Getty Images; 8:
MPI/Stringer/Getty Images; 9: Science and Society/Superstock, Inc.; 10: Heritage Image
Partnership Ltd/Alamy Images; 11 top: Bettmann/Corbis Images; 11 bottom: Three Lions/
Stringer/Getty Images; 12: Sean Pavone/Shutterstock, Inc.; 13: Rolf Schulten/imagebr/
imageBROKER/Superstock, Inc.; 14: Cordelia Molloy/Science Source; 15: Brookhaven National
Laboratory; 16: Alexis Duclos/Getty Images; 17: imageBROKER/Superstock, Inc.; 18: Kyodo/
Newscom; 19: Pete Seaward/Getty Images; 20: Bloomberg/Getty Images; 22: Owen
Franken/Corbis Images; 23: Raphael Gaillarde/Getty Images; 24: epa european pressphoto
agency b.v./Alamy Images; 25 top: LIU JIN/Stringer/Getty Images; 25 bottom: Xinhua/
Alamy Images; 26: secablue/iStockphoto; 27: Chandan Khanna/Stringer/Getty Images; 28
top: North Wind Picture Archives; 28-29 bottom: jeremy sutton-hibbert/Alamy Images; 29 top:
Tampa Bay Times/Zuma Press; 30: ZUMA Press, Inc./Alamy Images; 31: High Speed Rail
Authority/ZUMApress/Newscom; 32: Agencja Fotograficzna Caro/Alamy Images; 34: Benjamin
Lowy/Getty Images; 35: Agencja Fotograficzna Caro/Alamy Images; 36: Drew Galloway;
38: UrbanEye/Alamy Images; 39: Bloomberg/Getty Images; 40 top: Aurora Photos/Alamy
Images; 40-41 bottom: Allan Baxter/Getty Images; 41 top: Stefano Politi Markovina/Alamy
Images; 42: Mark Hunt/Media Bakery; 43: Carlos Barria/Reuters; 44: JTB PhotoUIG Universal
Images Group/Newscom; 46: Stephen Bisgrove/Alamy Images; 47: Media Bakery; 48: Alain
Le Garsmeur/Getty Images; 49 top: Richard B. Levine/Newscom; 49 bottom: Green Stock
Media/Alamy Images; 50: Education Images/Getty Images; 51: Bernd Mellmann/Alamy
Images; 52: JTB Photo/Getty Images; 53: Lee Snlder/Alamy Images; 54 left: ClassicStock.
com/Superstock, Inc.; 54 right: Frank H. Conlon/Star Ledger/Corbis Images; 55: matthew
siddons/Shutterstock, Inc.; 56: New York Daily News Archive/Getty Images; 57: Charles
Platiau/Reuters; 58: DBURKE/Alamy Images; 59: David Lyon/Alamy Images.

LIBRARY OF CONGRESS CATALOGING-IN-PUBLICATION DATA
Otfinoski, Steven, author.
 High-speed trains : from concept to consumer / by Steven Otfinoski.
   pages cm. — (Calling all innovators : a career for you)
 Summary: "Learn about the history of high-speed rail travel and find out what it takes to make
it in this exciting career field." — Provided by publisher.
 Includes bibliographical references and index.
 ISBN 978-0-531-21899-0 (library binding) — ISBN 978-0-531-21917-1 (pbk.)
 1. High speed trains—Juvenile literature. 2. Railroad engineers—Juvenile literature. 3.
Railroad engineering—Vocational guidance—Juvenile literature. I. Title. II. Series: Calling all
innovators.
 TF1455.084 2015
 385.3'7—dc23   2015002479

All rights reserved. Published in 2016 by Children's Press, an imprint of Scholastic Inc.
Printed in the United States of America 113

1 2 3 4 5 6 7 8 9 10 R 25 24 23 22 21 20 19 18 17 16

S cience, technology, engineering, arts, and math are the fields that drive innovation. Whether they are finding ways to make our lives easier or developing the latest entertainment, the people who work in these fields are changing the world for the better. Do you have what it takes to join the ranks of today's greatest innovators? Read on to discover if a career in the exciting world of high-speed train transportation is for you.

TABLE *of* CONTENTS

Early trains were powered by steam engines.

A train exits the underwater tunnel between Great Britain and France.

Mechanics work on the underside of a high-speed train in Germany.

Many high-speed train companies offer a range of services to passengers.

EXHAUST STEAM
RELEASED INTO AIR

*Steam-powered trains changed the way
people thought about transportation.*

WHEELS SHAPED TO
MOVE ALONG TRACKS

1

SPEEDING THROUGH TIME

The year is 1804. The place is South Wales, in Great Britain. People have gathered along a track to watch a strange new machine. It looks like a barrel on wheels. Water in the barrel is heated by a coal fire beneath it. This turns it into steam. The steam moves a **piston** attached to the machine's wheels, making them turn. Because of all the steam that puffs out of the machine, its inventor, Richard Trevithick, calls it the Puffing Devil.

The spectators are impressed, but not by the vehicle's speed. At about 4 miles (6 kilometers) per hour, the Puffing Devil moves so slowly that Trevithick can walk alongside it without falling behind. The amazing thing about this machine is that it can move along the track without being pushed or pulled by an animal. The Puffing Devil is the first vehicle to move under its own power. Before long, steam-powered trains would become a widely used method of transportation.

LOW-SPEED LANDMARKS

1825	1850	1869	1895
George Stephenson's Stockton and Darlington Railway offers the first regular passenger steam train service in England.	Congress makes the first federal land grants for the development of railroads in the United States.	The first transcontinental U.S. railroad line is completed at Promontory, Utah, on May 10.	The Baltimore and Ohio Railroad begins offering the world's first electric train service.

STEAM TRAINS

At first, Trevithick's train was little more than a curiosity. However, in the decades ahead, steam trains were improved to the point where they could carry many passengers at speeds far beyond anything possible at the time.

By 1850, steam trains were the dominant form of transportation in many parts of the world. They carried passengers from city to city, state to state, and even country to country. The first transcontinental railroad in the United States was completed in 1869 by the Union Pacific and Central Pacific Railroads. It allowed people to travel easily from one end of the country to the other.

As tracks were laid all around the world, engineers and inventors continued finding ways to make steam-powered trains even faster. By the end of the 1800s, some trains were able to reach speeds of up to 126 miles per hour (203 kph).

Central Pacific Railroad workers lay tracks in Nevada in 1868.

Rudolf Diesel's engine did not burn as much fuel as earlier engines.

THE AGE OF DIESEL

Wood, coal, or sometimes oil was burned in a train's engine. The fire heated tubes of water, and the water was turned into steam. As the steam expanded, it moved the engine's pistons. The pistons drove rods and cranks that turned the wheels of the train.

Steam power was not a very **efficient** use of fuel. Only 10 percent of the energy released from burning coal was used to propel trains. The other 90 percent was given off as excess heat. In 1892, the German scientist Rudolf Diesel invented a new type of engine that was later named for him. Though they still relied on burning coal, diesel engines were about 40 percent more efficient than steam engines. By the 1950s, most railroad companies in North America and Europe had switched from steam to diesel engines.

PAST MARVELS

New Yorkers ride a subway train in 1901.

ELECTRIC TRAINS

Though diesel engines were an improvement over steam, they were far from perfect. As electricity became more common throughout the world, some engineers began searching for ways to use it to power trains. The first electric trains appeared in the 1880s. The electricity came from a rail located in the tracks below the train or, more commonly, from wires that ran above the train. Electric trains were cleaner, quieter, easier to operate, and faster than steam or diesel trains.

AROUND THE WORLD

Germany was the first nation to use electric trains, but others soon followed. Because they had to be connected to power lines, electric trains were most practical within urban areas where electrical systems were already in place. This made them the perfect trains for the new underground mass transit systems being built in London and New York City. These trains were called subways.

DIESEL MEETS ELECTRIC

While electric trains offered many advantages, they could not go everywhere a steam or diesel train could. In 1924, an American engineer helped solve this problem by combining a diesel engine with an electric motor. This new invention was soon put to work in trains.

In a diesel-electric train, pistons are powered by burning fuel. Their movement turns a generator or alternator which produces electricity to power an electric motor. This motor moves the train's wheels. Diesel-electric trains use less fuel and need less maintenance than steam or diesel-only trains. They also eliminate the need for overhead wires or electric rails. As a result, a diesel-electric train could travel great distances at higher speeds than city subways. The *Pioneer Zephyr*, the first

The Pioneer Zephyr *was capable of reaching top speeds in excess of 100 miles per hour (161 kph).*

diesel-electric train in the United States, began service between Chicago, Illinois, and Denver, Colorado, in 1934. Over this distance of more than 1,000 miles (1,609 km), it ran at an average speed of just over 77 miles per hour (124 kph). Two years later, it set a long-distance speed record of 83.3 miles per hour (134 kph). By the 1950s, diesel-electric trains had become the standard for train travel. ✳

Riders wait for a train on the first subway line in the United States.

SLEEK SHAPE ALLOWS TRAIN
TO SLICE THROUGH AIR

A Shinkansen train passes in front of Mt. Fuji as it barrels across the Japanese countryside.

JAPAN'S BULLET TRAIN

The era of the high-speed train truly began in 1964. That year, a new railroad line called the Shinkansen (Japanese for "new super express") began service between the Japanese cities of Tokyo and Osaka. The fully electrified train made the 320-mile (515 km) journey in 3 hours and 10 minutes, reaching a top speed of 130 miles per hour (209 kph). This was nearly an hour faster than the time traditional trains would take.

Because it did not rely on burning fuel, the "bullet train" gave off much less pollution than cars did. In order to prevent accidents, routes were built on elevated land to avoid contact with people or cars. In fact, the train has maintained a perfect safety record for more than 50 years, with not a single death due to collision or derailment.

PROBLEMS AND CHALLENGES

Japan's bullet train was not without its problems. Because it ran solely on electricity, a wirelike device called a **pantograph** was attached to each car's roof to make contact with electric cables running overhead along the track. The noise the pantograph made was annoying to people who lived or worked near the line. Also, the powerful vibrations from the train blasting through tunnels caused nearby buildings to shake as if struck by an earthquake.

Mechanical engineers redesigned the nose of the train to make it long and sleek, like the beak of a bird. This decreased the pressure when it passed through the tunnels and reduced the noise by more than 25 percent. Since 1964, the bullet train network has grown to connect many parts of Japan. Today, the country's trains reach a top speed of 185 miles per hour (298 kph) and serve more than 150 million people each year.

Most electric trains still rely on pantographs to supply them with power today.

ELECTRIC CABLES

PANTOGRAPH TRANSFERS ELECTRICITY FROM CABLES TO TRAIN

13

FIRST THINGS FIRST

Magnetic forces of the same type repel each other.

MIGHTY MAGNETS

The power of magnets has been known since the beginning of recorded history. These incredible objects produce fields of energy that can repel or attract other objects. They have long fascinated scientists, and countless innovators have found ways to put them to practical use. In 1922, German scientist Hermann Kemper first had the idea of using magnets to power a train.

FLOATING ABOVE THE RAILS

Two American engineers, Gordon Danby and James Powell—working independently of Kemper—came up with a similar concept in 1960. They called their proposed technology "maglev," a combination of the words "magnetic levitation." Their train would have powerful magnets on the underside of its cars. The magnetic field created by electric wires in the track would, they believed, create enough force to lift the train above the track and at the same time propel it forward.

AHEAD OF ITS TIME

Maglev technology took the concept of high-speed train travel to a new level. Because the train would float above the track, there would be no **friction** between wheels and tracks. In fact, there would be no need for wheels at all. Or an engine. Maglev would not need to burn fuel to operate and would give off no air pollution. In addition, maglev trains would have only a few moving parts, so there would be little need for maintenance. The concept was brilliant, but making it a reality would present many challenges. Much to the frustration of Danby and Powell, American railroad companies and the U.S. government showed little interest in their concept. The idea would not be developed for several decades. ✳

Gordon Danby (left) and James Powell (right) were not recognized for their amazing achievement until many years after they first developed the ideas behind maglev technology.

EUROPEAN MODELS

The success of Japan's bullet train inspired other countries to pursue high-speed rail service, especially in Europe. France introduced its first high-speed trains in 1967. They ran at a speed of 125 miles per hour (201 kph). Great Britain's British Rail launched its InterCity 125 line in 1976, running at the same speed. Both of these rail systems operated on the same tracks as slower traditional trains. This made it difficult for the newer trains to maintain top speeds. Europe's first fully dedicated high-speed track appeared in Italy in 1977. The train ran between the cities of Rome and Florence and reached a top speed of 160 miles per hour (257 kph).

In 1981, France unveiled its Train à Grande Vitesse (Very Fast Train) system, known as TGV. The first TGV route ran between the cities of Paris and Lyons. It made the trip in 2 hours and 30 minutes, reaching a top speed of 168 miles per hour (270 kph). Over the next two decades, TGV would expand to form one of the world's most extensive high-speed train networks. It not only crossed France but also carried passengers to and from Belgium, the Netherlands, and other neighboring countries.

TGV trains allow for rapid transit through France and the surrounding area.

An ICE train travels out of Frankfurt, Germany.

GERMANY TAKES THE LEAD

Germany's entry into high-speed rail was delayed by legal difficulties. However, once aboard, it took a leading role in the new technology. Its InterCity Express (ICE) began in 1991, traveling between major cities such as Hamburg, Hanover, and Frankfurt. It soon began carrying passengers to Switzerland and Austria as well. However, a design mistake led to tragedy. In 1998, an ICE train derailed near Eschede, Germany, killing 101 passengers and injuring another 80. The cause was found to be faulty wheels. German engineers redesigned the train wheels immediately, correcting the problem.

Other Asian countries joined in the high-speed train industry. South Korea began operating its first high-speed train line in 2004, running between the cities of Seoul and Busan. Taiwan launched its first high-speed line in 2007 between Taipei and Kaohsiung.

Amtrak's Acela Express was a pioneer of high-speed train service in the United States.

THE UNITED STATES GETS IN THE RACE

The United States was slow to get into the business of high-speed trains. There were several reasons for this. Unlike cities in Europe and Japan, large American cities are far apart. This makes lines dedicated to high-speed trains much more expensive to build. Commercial train companies were unable to pay for construction without the support of state and federal governments, and lawmakers were reluctant to lay out the needed funds.

Finally, in 2000, Amtrak launched its Acela Express line in the Northeast Corridor. The name Acela is a combination of the words "accelerate" and "excellent." Its top speed of 150 miles per hour (241 kph) made it the fastest passenger train in the United States, but it lagged behind Europe and Asia's fastest trains.

THE CALIFORNIA CONNECTION

In 2010, California received federal funding to begin building its own high-speed rail system. The California High-Speed Rail Authority plans to build an 800-mile (1,287 km) line from San Diego to Sacramento with a bullet train that will travel 218 miles per hour (351 kph). At a total cost of $68 billion, the California line will be the nation's largest **infrastructure** project to date. Not only will it offer new mobility to millions of people traveling across the state, but it will also reduce the state's need for oil—which provides gasoline for cars—by more than 12 million barrels a year.

The ambitious project has hit numerous snags in its early stages. Politicians have argued over its practicality. Engineering the route across a varied terrain that includes mountains will not be easy. However, many Californians are committed to the project and are confident that it can succeed.

Highway traffic in Los Angeles, California, and the surrounding area is often extremely heavy.

EURO
TUNNEL

Construction of the Channel
Tunnel took about six years.

3208

2

FASTER AND FASTER

efore 1994, if you wanted to cross the Strait of Dover from Great Britain to France, you had to take a ferry or an airplane. Not anymore. That year, the Channel Tunnel, better known as the Chunnel, opened, providing high-speed train travel between the two countries. Trains zoom through tubes on separate tracks in each direction with a third tube for service needs. The 20-minute ride spans 31 miles (50 km). For more than two-thirds of the route, the tunnels are completely underwater at an average depth of 164 feet (50 meters). Moving at 99 miles per hour (159 kph), it is the fastest underground train system in the world.

The Chunnel is the first direct connection between Britain and the European continent. It is a good example of the engineering genius and technical skill that make high-speed trains the gold standard for mass transportation around the world today.

RECORD-BREAKING SPEEDS

1964	1977	1990	2003
The first Japanese bullet train achieves a top speed of 130 miles per hour (209 kph).	Italy's first high-speed train between Rome and Florence reaches 160 miles per hour (257 kph).	France's TGV Atlantique train records a top speed of 322 miles per hour (518 kph).	Japan's maglev test train hits 361 miles per hour (581 kph), a world record as of 2015.

A CONTINENT UNITED

The Shinkansen celebrated 50 years of service on October 4, 2014. When it began operating in 1964, there were no other high-speed trains in the world. Today, 26 countries have high-speed train service or are developing it. Europe is especially well connected by high-speed service. A passenger can travel almost anywhere in the western part of the continent using high-speed trains. The service is fast, comfortable, and affordable. France's TGV continues to be one of the premiere high-speed train services, and it currently has three big, new projects under way. The most ambitious is a high-speed line from Tours to Bordeaux along the Atlantic coast. Set to open in August 2017, the route will include 188 miles (303 km) of dedicated tracks that will cross 24 new bridges over rivers and valleys.

Germany's ICE system continues to forge ahead as well. While all other European systems rely on electrified wheeled trains, Germany's new Transrapid system uses maglev technology. A test track in the city of Emsland runs for 19.6 miles (31.5 km) and has reached speeds of up to 340 miles per hour (547 kph).

Passengers wait to board a high-speed train from Paris, France, to London, England.

A Spanish AVE train travels between the cities of Seville and Madrid.

SPAIN AND ITALY

Today, Spain's Alta Velocidad Española (AVE) trains make up the largest high-speed network in Europe. At speeds of up to 193 miles per hour (311 kph), these trains can travel from Madrid in central Spain to Barcelona on the east coast in less than three hours. The network's line from Madrid to Seville in the south is so reliable that it guarantees arrival within five minutes of scheduled time or makes a full refund to passengers. It has had to refund money on only a small number of its runs.

Italy's Alta Velocità high-speed trains first ran between Rome and Florence in 1977. Today the network operates one main line from Turin to Salerno that includes stops in Milan, Bologna, and Rome. A second line is under construction between Turin and Venice, Italy's famed city on the water.

SLOPED SHAPE REDUCES
AIR RESISTANCE

An experimental maglev train in Japan is able to travel between the cities of Tokyo and Nagoya, at speeds more than twice as fast as a traditional bullet train.

THE MAGLEVS OF ASIA

Maglevs are likely the high-speed trains of the future, and Japan, China, and South Korea are already enjoying the benefits of this cutting-edge technology. While the bullet train is still the dominant form of high-speed transportation in Japan, the Central Japan Railway has been testing a maglev system since 1997. Its Linear High-Speed Train has reached speeds of up to 361 miles per hour (581 kph) in tests. That's about twice the speed of a jet airplane on takeoff.

Construction of the Chuo (Central) Shinkansen, a maglev train that will run 178 miles (287 km) from Tokyo to Nagoya, is set to begin in 2015. Because trains moved by magnets must run in straight lines to keep the magnetic field active, they cannot go around natural obstacles. Tunnels must be built to go through mountains. The work will be difficult, and the route is not expected to be open for business until 2027. But the wait may be well worth it. Engineers predict that the train will run at a speed of 300 miles per hour (483 kph), making the journey in 40 minutes. This is an hour less than a bullet train takes.

Passengers look out the window of a high-speed maglev train on the way to Pudong International Airport in Shanghai, China.

SHANGHAI EXPRESS

China has a maglev line in place between the center of Shanghai and Pudong International Airport. The train whizzes 4 inches (10 centimeters) above the concrete track at a speed of 268 miles per hour (431 kph), making the 19-mile (31 km) trip in just 7.5 minutes. The Chinese want to expand maglev service much further. In 2014, scientists working at Southwest Jiaotong University built an experimental maglev that could potentially reach a speed of 1,800 miles per hour (2,897 kph)! While this super maglev is far from becoming a reality, its inventors think it could eventually be used for military purposes and even space launches.

SOUTH KOREA AND RUSSIA

In July 2014, South Korea launched the world's third passenger maglev train service. However, it is not very fast compared to other trains. The unpiloted train runs from Incheon International Airport to the city of Yongyu, a distance of 3.8 miles (6 km), at a top speed of only 68 miles per hour (109 kph). In time, the South Koreans hope to extend the line and make it a circular route.

Meanwhile, Russia is planning a maglev rail system between Moscow and Vladivostok in Siberia. Experts believe that maglev trains, because they are frictionless and don't touch the tracks, will be far less affected by the route's harsh northern weather conditions than more conventional trains are. ☀

South Korea's first maglev train allows for easy transportation to Incheon International Airport, the nation's largest airport.

Trains must travel almost 5 miles (8 km) to cross the Oresund Bridge between Sweden and Denmark.

A HIGH-SPEED WORLD

High-speed trains are gaining ground across the globe. Northern Europe is starting to catch up with its neighbors to the south. Sweden's government-run SJ trains are relatively slow at 124 miles per hour (200 kph), but they travel to most of the nation's major cities. They also cross over the Oresund Bridge, the longest road and rail bridge in Europe, to neighboring Denmark. The overnight train to northern Sweden covers nearly 414 miles (666 km), making it one of the longest high-speed routes in Europe. Norway has one of the shortest high-speed routes—40 miles (64 km) from Oslo Airport to the city's hub. More lines are planned in the next two decades. Finland opened its Allegro high-speed train line between Helsinki, the capital, and St. Petersburg, Russia, in December 2010. The trip takes three and a half hours.

PLANS FOR THE FUTURE

Many other countries are planning to add high-speed trains in the near future. For example, a 322-mile (518 km) route between Rio de Janeiro and São Paulo is planned in Brazil. Argentina is looking to build a 440-mile (708 km) high-speed train linking the cities of Buenos Aires, Rosario, and Córdoba. Currently, no rail service exists between these major hubs, and the main transportation between them is a four-lane highway.

India has one of the largest rail networks in the world but no high-speed trains. Indian Railways set a goal of having a train that can run between 99 and 124 miles per hour (159 and 200 kph) on conventional tracks. In July 2014, one of its trains reached a speed of 99 miles per hour (159 kph) on a track between New Delhi and Agra.

Africa is the only major continent other than Australia without a high-speed rail system. But in 2010, South Africa announced plans for a 448-mile (721 km) high-speed rail between Johannesburg and Durban. The route goes through the Drakensberg mountain range, a formidable obstacle for the project. In North Africa, Algeria and Morocco have plans for more modest high-speed lines.

Billions of people travel on trains each year in India.

FROM THIS TO THAT

George Pullman helped make long-distance rail travel comfortable for passengers.

A COMFORTABLE JOURNEY

During the golden age of steam trains, wealthy passengers often traveled in luxury. In 1865, inventor George Pullman perfected an elaborate train compartment that could easily be transformed from a seated car by day to a comfortable sleeping car by night. Pullman also improved dining cars, and his luxurious parlor cars gave passengers a place to sit, visit, and watch the passing landscape.

CHANGING TIMES

By the 1950s, trains were facing stiff competition from airlines and automobiles. Fewer people rode trains, and service and **amenities** declined. With the appearance of high-speed trains in the 1960s and '70s in Europe and Asia, passenger count began to rise again. Many of the luxuries of the past returned, and new ones appeared as well. Today, Japanese bullet trains offer white-glove service and elegant boxed meals. Seats can turn 180 degrees to give passengers

a front view of the passing landscape at all times. More expensive cars offer more personal space and better service.

EUROPEAN ELEGANCE

Today's European high-speed trains offer many perks. Café cars serve everything from snacks and beverages to elaborate three-course dinners, often with waiter service. German ICE train cars are air-conditioned in summer. Passengers can pass the time watching films and TV programs on video screens or listening to

A variety of snacks are available to purchase on Shinkansen trains.

Passengers enjoy breakfast in a dining car aboard a Canadian train.

different kinds of music on audio systems. Wireless Internet access is offered in many cars, and conference rooms are available for businesspeople who want to hold meetings while traveling. On Swedish SJ trains, families with children can use special play cars where kids can enjoy themselves without bothering other passengers. On today's high-speed trains, passengers enjoy the ride in comfort.

DIMINISHED EXPECTATIONS

The United States continues to lag behind other nations in the high-speed train game. Hopes were high when Amtrak announced a multimillion-dollar overhaul of its Acela trains in 2012. That year, the company produced a plan to replace the trains with new ones that could eventually travel 220 miles per hour (354 kph) along the Northeast Corridor. But within a few months, the predicted speed was lowered to 160 miles per hour (258 kph). Amtrak spokespeople argued that the infrastructure of the crowded, densely populated Northeast Corridor prohibited trains from traveling any faster. In addition, while Acela is popular, not everyone can afford it. Tickets are expensive, and most passengers are business travelers.

The proposed California high-speed system, which broke ground in Fresno in January 2015, is promising. However, it is a long way from becoming a reality.

An Acela train pulls into a station in Boston, Massachusetts.

This artist's impression shows what high-speed rail lines in California may one day look like.

TEXAS LEADS THE WAY

Recently the state of Texas announced plans to build a high-speed rail service between Dallas and Houston. The 240-mile (386 km) route is a popular commuter path traveled by more than 50,000 workers weekly by car or plane. The estimated cost of the railway is $10 billion. Construction costs will be low thanks to flat country that is sparsely populated. Texas Central Railway is committed to the project and hopes to have it up and running by 2021. "Until and unless someone builds and operates such a high-speed train in the United States on a true, dedicated corridor," claims the company's chairman Richard Lawless, "no one in the United States is going to understand what it is all about."

An ICE train is assembled
at a factory in Germany.

CHAPTER THREE

WORKING ON THE RAILROAD

A s more high-speed rail systems open in the United States, thousands of jobs will need to be filled to build and operate them. Urban planners and railroad engineers will be needed to develop and design the routes the new trains will take and to locate the best places for stations. Skilled workers will be needed to construct the trains, rail lines, and stations. Once the high-speed trains are up and running, other workers will be needed to operate and maintain them and serve the needs of passengers.

In 2012, American railroad companies employed 113,800 people. That number will continue to grow as new high-speed train lines crisscross cities, towns, and states. If high-speed train travel is indeed the mass transportation of the future, it could become a major employer in the nation.

TRAIN STATION MILESTONES

1910	1939	1998	2009
New York City's grand Pennsylvania Station opens for business.	Los Angeles, California's Union Station is completed at a cost of $11 million.	Grand Central Station reopens in New York City.	The breathtaking Liège-Guillemins TGV Station opens in Belgium.

Workers construct a high-speed railroad bridge in Nanjing, China.

PLANNING A COURSE

Old, conventional railroad lines will not do for the high-speed trains of tomorrow. New, dedicated lines will be necessary. This poses a challenge to railroad companies. Urban planners need to find the best, most practical routes for these trains through cities and towns and across states. Planners will need to work with government officials to secure public lands for the rails. They must also meet with businesspeople and residents who own private lands that the rails would pass over. They will need to make certain their railroads meet legal requirements to gain the **right-of-way** on these lands.

Mechanical engineers will plan and design the railways and their paths from station to station. They will also design the trains, whether electric or maglev, for speed, efficiency, and safety. Once the plans, routes, and designs are in place, construction will begin. An army of skilled workers and technicians will build the trains on assembly lines. Welders, electricians, carpenters, and construction workers will build the stations. Project managers will oversee their work to ensure that it is done correctly and on time.

RUNNING A TRAIN

Once the tracks, trains, and stations are completed, the trains are ready to roll. A full crew of workers is needed to operate and maintain the trains and serve their many passengers. Locomotive engineers drive the trains, stopping at each station to let off and take on passengers. They must be able to maintain a consistent speed to keep the train on schedule, but also be able to slow down or stop the train when its control systems require it. To help them know what lies ahead, they keep in constant communication via radio with dispatchers who provide updates on track conditions, delays, and schedule changes. Engineering crews at maintenance bases receive information about the train electronically while it is traveling and assist the locomotive engineers to keep the train running.

Brake operators help **couple** and decouple train cars when necessary. They may do this work in the railroad yard before or after a run. In other cases, they travel on a train as part of the crew. Signal operators set up and maintain signals along the rails and in the rail yards. Signals are critical to safety, letting engineers know when they need to slow down or make way for another train. From centralized operations centers, dispatchers control the switches on the main tracks that allow trains to move from one track to another.

Mechanics work on the underside of a German ICE train.

Drew Galloway is chief of planning and performance for Amtrak's Northeast Corridor, which runs between Boston, Massachusetts, and Washington, D.C. He believes strongly in an integrated train system, and that the Northeast Corridor, where Acela operates, is the greatest example of that integration.

When did you first realize that you wanted to work in the train industry? As a kid, I was fascinated by all kinds of transportation, but especially trains. There were train lines near my home in northwest New Jersey. I watched the trains pass by, going to places I could only imagine. I felt the glamour of the passenger trains and the importance of the freight trains carrying all kinds of goods. As I grew older, I came to realize that the railroad . . . involved lots of elements—engineering, operations, and finance among them. They are a complete shop, unlike airlines and bus companies. The airlines are not responsible for the air routes and the buses for the roads they travel on. The railroads are responsible for everything, and I found that challenging.

What kinds of classes did you take in college that prepared you for a career in rail transportation? In college, I majored in economics. Studying economics helped prepare me for the flexibility needed in the train business. Nothing stays the same. It's always changing, and you have to be able to adapt. I also took courses in finance and transportation law, which have proved helpful.

What did you learn in other jobs you held in school that helped you in your career? One summer job I held before I graduated from college was working for a marine international shipping firm. I learned how a business culture evolved over time and how goods travel back and forth. I also learned the importance of attention to detail and perseverance, two qualities that will help you in any career. My first job out of college was working for a freight railroad company.

What rail project have you worked on that you're especially proud of? Before I went to work at Amtrak, I worked for New Jersey Transit. I was a project manager on improving train service between Manhattan and New Jersey. It was a huge challenge and involved changing 200 train schedules and 500 crew assignments. It was a two-to-three-year effort, and it increased rail service in New Jersey to 30,000 trips a day. I'm very proud that it succeeded so well.

It takes a team of people to create and run a railway. Does working as part of a team come naturally to you, and how do you handle the other team members when you're the boss? Let me say that many people's first instinct is to take the easy way and do a job your own way, regardless of other people. I learned quickly in the train business that doesn't work. The collaborative process is better, and you end up with a better product and a much better outcome.

What would your dream project be if you were given unlimited resources? I'm working on a dream project right now. It is planning new tunnels to run under the Hudson River in New York City. Once finished, this project will increase the number of trains running in the Northeast Corridor from 450 a day to 1,000 a day. It is an ambitious project that will take a decade to complete, but it will create the railroad footprint in this region for the next 100 years. That's exciting!

What advice would you give to young people who want to work in the field of high-speed trains? I would tell them to learn every aspect of the train business—the technology, development, finance, and the environmental impact. All these are important to creating a viable rail system that will serve the public well. Amtrak and other rail companies have summer jobs and internships available to young people. They range from working on the tracks to working in an office. The opportunities are there. ✴

SERVING PASSENGERS

Conductors are the captains of the train. They open the train's doors at each station stop, assist passengers who need help getting aboard, and signal the engineer to leave the station when it is safe to do so. They also collect tickets, answer passengers' questions about schedules and other concerns, and deal with unruly passengers. They announce each upcoming stop to give passengers time to get off the train at their destination or make a connection with another train.

Conductors also supervise other workers on the train. Among these workers are the food servers who run the café cars selling food and beverages to passengers. If a train runs overnight and provides sleeping accommodations for passengers, there will also be attendants and maids to see to their needs and comfort. Maintenance workers keep the train clean and in good running order.

A conductor collects tickets on a high-speed train in Shanghai, China.

209	8:20	Shin-ōsaka	17	Non-Reserved
13	8:30	Hakata	19	Non-Reserved Car No.1-3
157	8:40	Hakata	18	Non-Reserved Car No.1-3
317	8:47	Shin-ōsaka	17	Non-Reserved Car No.1-3

Max やまびこ	
あさま	515号
はやて・こまち	75号
とき	361号
やまびこ	49号
あさま	517号

Keeping a busy train station running smoothly can be a difficult job.

IN THE STATION

Train stations are the hubs where passengers begin and end their journeys. Among the many people who work in train stations are station managers, ticket agents, and maintenance workers. Many stations offer a variety of shops and other services to passengers. This requires a wide range of additional workers.

Many railroad companies, such as Amtrak, have their own security or police forces. These officers patrol stations to ensure the safety of passengers and investigate any criminal activity or suspicious behavior. Many of these railroad police are veterans of the military. "My favorite part is knowing that each day when I go home, I know that I've helped," says one station police officer who was recruited from the U.S. Army. "I've protected the passengers and the other employees."

THE ARTISTIC SIDE

Santiago Calatrava is the architect behind Belgium's Liège-Guillemins TGV Station.

STATION TO STATION

Designed for speed, high-speed trains have a streamlined beauty. Similarly, many of the stations they pass through are created with an eye for beauty. Perhaps no modern-day train station is as artistically stunning as the Liège-Guillemins TGV Station in Liège, Belgium. Designed by **architect** Santiago Calatrava, the station is a monumental structure of steel, glass, and white concrete. Its most notable feature is a giant arch that is 525 feet (160 m) long and 105 feet (32 m) high. The station, which

opened in September 2009, is a major hub for passengers traveling on high-speed trains to Germany, Luxembourg, France, and the Netherlands.

OLD AND NEW

Like other buildings, train stations are often updated to make them more modern. A good example is the Atocha Train Station in Madrid, Spain. The original station burned down in the 1890s and was rebuilt with a new design by several architects, including Gustave Eiffel, the

creator of Paris's famed Eiffel Tower. The station was updated again in 1992 with a new design by architect Rafael Moneo. Moneo's design combined the old and the new. It even added a tropical garden covering 43,060 square feet (4,000 sq m). The Atocha is the biggest train station in Madrid and a main center for the high-speed AVE trains that cross Spain. It is currently undergoing even further changes that will make it look more like an airport than a train station, with separate terminals for arrivals and departures.

Belgium's Liège-Guillemins TGV Station is known for its beautiful appearance.

Atocha Train Station in Madrid, Spain, is home to gardens that provide it with a unique look.

PRESERVING THE PAST

In the United States, some railroad companies are remembering their rich heritage and the role trains played in the nation's history. In 2006, Amtrak started the Great American Stations Project. Its purpose is to educate towns and cities about their local train stations and help them find ways to preserve and protect them. One example is the one-story station in Wolf Point, Montana. It was built in 1963 with a wolf sculpture on one wall to honor the community's role in trapping and trading. ✳

Mechanical engineers attend college to learn how to design and build machines.

EDUCATION

There are jobs in the world of high-speed trains for people with almost every level of education. A college degree is required for urban planners or mechnical engineers in the railroad industry. Locomotive engineers and conductors must have a high school diploma. Many other jobs, such as brakemen and maintenance men, require no formal education. The biggest requirement for these jobs is a willingness to work hard and learn new skills.

Many railroad companies provide on-the-job training programs for recently hired workers. Smaller, regional railroads often send new employees to a central training facility or, in some cases, to training programs held at industrial schools or community colleges. Such training programs often combine hands-on experience with classroom instruction and can last from several weeks to a few months.

FURTHER TRAINING

Because of the enormous responsibility their jobs entail, locomotive engineers and train conductors receive especially rigorous training. Some engineers first work as conductors, learning all aspects of the train. Once accepted as engineers, they work side by side with experienced engineers for several months. During this time, they will learn every stretch of a route and any peculiarities of the track. In the United States, they must then pass a test to become certified by the Federal Railroad Administration (FRA). If an engineer should be moved at any time to a new route, the training process starts over and recertification is required. Engineers also take refresher courses on a regular basis to keep their skills sharp.

Conductor trainees in the United States attend classes and receive field instruction, which usually lasts about 16 weeks. At the end of this time, they take a written exam.

Operating a train is a high-pressure job that requires careful training.

High-speed trains cross a wide variety of terrain all over the world.

MAKING THE JOURNEY

High-speed trains come in many shapes and sizes. Some cover routes that are hundreds of miles long, and others travel only a short distance before reaching their destination. Some travel at a speed of several hundred miles per hour, while others zip along at 150 miles per hour (241 kph) or less. But the people who work on these trains all share some things in common: attention to safety and efficiency, thorough maintenance of their trains, and care for the needs of the millions of passengers who travel on their trains every year. The trains themselves may zoom to get you where you need to go, but the many workers who operate and serve on them take their time making sure every journey is safe, comfortable, and efficient. Let's take a ride on a high-speed train. All aboard!

AMERICAN PASSENGER TRAINS THROUGH THE YEARS

1971	1976	2000	2010
Amtrak is created to nationalize passenger trains in the United States.	Congress establishes Conrail to save and consolidate seven major northeastern train lines.	Amtrak's Acela service begins operation in the Northeast Corridor.	The California High-Speed Rail Authority announces plans to build a high-speed rail line between San Francisco and Los Angeles.

IN THE YARD

You are on your way to Union Station in New Haven, Connecticut. You are going to catch an Acela Express high-speed train to Providence, Rhode Island, to visit friends. The ride will be about 85 minutes long. It is just one part of the train's complete route between Boston, Massachusetts, and Washington, D.C. All you had to do to be ready for the trip was pack a bag and get to the station. The preparations the train workers went through to ready the train for you were far more complex. The night before, the train was given a thorough examination at the rail yard near the main station in Boston. It was serviced and cleaned, and the electrical and mechanical systems were inspected. Any necessary repairs or adjustments were done before the train left the yard.

The following morning, the conductor, engineer, and crew arrive to begin the first run of the day. Before passengers can begin boarding, the conductor reads through the train orders and checks the timetable and any other written instructions from the dispatcher, the worker who oversees the departure of the trains. Afterward, all is finally ready for passengers to come aboard.

A maintenance worker cleans the front window of a high-speed train in Italy.

Business travelers often use their time aboard trains to get work done.

ON BOARD FOR PROVIDENCE

By the time the train arrives in New Haven, it has already been to
Washington and is heading back. Some or all the crew has changed
along the way. This keeps the workers fresh and rested. There is
a soft swoosh as the train pulls into sight. As it draws closer, you
admire the sleek, streamlined look of the locomotive, typical of
high-speed trains around the world.

The doors glide open, and you step inside. The cars are wide and
spacious. The seats are soft and comfortable. You lift your bag into
an overhead bin and settle into a window seat. Many of the adults
around you are tapping away on their laptops, phones, and tablets.
This is definitely a train for businesspeople, who make up the
majority of the service's passengers. They are catching up on work
as they head to offices, meetings, or conferences. You, on the other
hand, have no work to do. You sit back in the comfortable seat to
enjoy the ride.

WHERE THE MAGIC HAPPENS

ON TRACK WITH AMTRAK

On May 7, 2011, National Train Day, Amtrak began a yearlong celebration of its 40th anniversary. Four commemorative locomotives and a special Exhibition Train toured the country. The rail service had plenty to celebrate. When it was founded in 1971, passenger train service in the United States had fallen on hard times and was in danger of disappearing entirely. Despite its ups and downs over the years, Amtrak has made rail service popular again in the United States. Today, it serves tens of thousands of passengers daily on hundreds of trains. New technology has allowed the company to offer such services as online ticketing, wireless Internet service on most trains, and the first high-speed train service in North America.

ACELA'S SUCCESS

Since starting service in the Northeast Corridor in 2000, Acela has had its successes and failures. While capable of reaching speeds of 165 miles per hour (266 kph), its trains have only reached

An Amtrak train passes through Chicago, Illinois, in 1979.

Online ticketing and ticket kiosks provide customers with a variety of options for purchasing train fares.

a maximum speed in regular services of 150 miles per hour (241 kph). Even lower speeds are common along portions of the route. The high density of population between Boston and Washington, D.C., and the need to share tracks with slower trains have caused the slowdown.

A BRIGHT FUTURE

Ridership on Acela continues to rise. In 2013, it carried 3.3 million passengers, making up 25 percent of all Amtrak customers. Train service between Washington, D.C., and New York has been so popular that several airlines have abandoned the route due to falling numbers of passengers. In addition, upgrades to

the route's tracks, especially along the Connecticut shoreline, will help to raise train speeds in the coming years. ✳

Acela trains will be a big part of Amtrak's future.

An Acela train passes through Providence, Rhode Island.

MOVING OUT

The doors close, and the train leaves the station. You are amazed by how quiet and smooth the ride is. The train is not moving too fast yet, maybe 70 miles per hour (113 kph). You don't mind, though, because the Connecticut coastline is a beautiful sight. The conductor smiles and asks for your ticket. You give it to her, and she swipes it with a handheld electronic scanner. The scanner gets information from the bar code on the ticket—your identity, where you boarded the train, your final destination, and any other important information. There is no more punching tickets like there was in the old days. If you have a smartphone, you can give the conductor your code without a paper ticket at all. From the information in the electronic scanner, the conductor can determine if there are any empty seats on the train that can be sold as needed en route.

SLOW BUT STEADY

As the train continues to chug along, the tracks twist and turn. However, you hardly feel the change in motion. As the conductor comes back through your car, you ask her how the ride can be so smooth. She explains that there is a tilting mechanism in the train's bed that stabilizes it on turns and keeps it level for passenger comfort. You tell her how you noticed that the train slows down during the turns. She explains that this is one of the things that keeps the Acela from reaching the high speeds it is capable of. Outdated bridges and overpasses that might be unsafe at high speeds are other places the train slows down. However, the conductor hints that the train won't go so slow for the entire trip. "Just wait until we get into Rhode Island," she says with a wink.

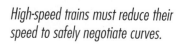
High-speed trains must reduce their speed to safely negotiate curves.

A TRAIN LIKE A PLANE

As you look around the car, you are surprised to notice that the train reminds you more of an airplane than any other train you've been on. It is more spacious and comfortable than the commuter trains you've ridden, and each seat has a foldout tray for food or to prop up a laptop. Inside the seat pocket below the tray is a brochure of safety instructions in case of an emergency. It also contains a menu of food and drinks you can buy from the café car. At the front of the car above the door is a digital screen with readouts. They provide updated information about safety issues, destinations, and other important topics. After a while, you feel like it's time to get up and explore the rest of the train.

On longer rides, it is common for train lines to offer full meals to passengers.

First-class seats are more comfortable than those in coach, but tickets are more expensive.

AN EXPLORING EXPEDITION

There are eight cars on your train—two cars for powering the train and six passenger cars. You are in one of the three business-class passenger cars. You walk back to see the other cars. The first is the café car. Here passengers can order food and drinks at a counter and then sit and enjoy their snacks while admiring the passing landscape through large windows. Next, you enter what is called the quiet car. Every Acela train has one. It is for passengers who want peace and quiet on their journey. Cell phone use is not allowed, and loud conversation is discouraged. The last car on your train is for first-class passengers. The seats are more luxurious than the ones in business class. Two servers bring complimentary food and drinks as well as newspapers and hot towels to the passengers at their seats. You decide that when you're older and you have a job, you will ride first class. You return to your seat and see you are passing through New London, Connecticut. Soon you'll be in Rhode Island.

LASTING CONTRIBUTIONS

THE CAPTAIN OF THE TRAIN

From the beginning of passenger train travel, the conductor has been the captain of the train. The engineer may make the train move, but it is the conductor who sees to most of the needs of the passengers, crew, and the train itself. During the early days of train travel in the United States, many conductors were former captains of steamboats or sailing ships. They brought their leadership and organizational skills to the trains. With their blue uniforms,

Throughout history, conductors have let passengers know when a train is preparing to leave the station.

A conductor collects tickets aboard a train in New Jersey.

conductor caps, and large gold pocket watches to keep track of departure and arrival times, they were a comforting presence to passengers.

STILL IN CHARGE

While some human workers, such as signalmen and even some engineers, have been replaced by automated technology, human conductors are still needed on today's high-speed passenger trains. Their duties continue to be important. They check passengers' tickets, take payment from those who didn't purchase tickets in advance, see to passengers' needs and safety, and answer questions about train times and stations. If a train carries freight, its conductors also oversee the loading and unloading of any cargo. In addition, conductors supervise crew members, especially the assistant conductors who work under them, and create reports detailing arrivals and departures and any unscheduled stops or delays.

MASTER CONDUCTORS

While conductors' jobs on passenger trains are safe despite rising automation, freight trains are a different matter. In 2014, Burlington Northern Santa Fe Railway, one of the nation's largest freight carriers, announced plans to begin using single-person crews on its trains. The engineer would run the train alone. All other crew members, including conductors, would be replaced by automation. A master conductor would be employed for multiple trains. He or she would ride around in a van and be on call to assist any train that had a problem. However, conductors and other railroad workers voted down this plan, calling it unsafe and dangerous. Engineers didn't like it either. As a result, conductors will remain on the nation's freight trains for the present. ✳

Conductors play an important role in the operation of freight trains as well as passenger trains.

An Acela train arrives at New York City's Pennsylvania Station on the line's first-ever trip from Washington, D.C.

DESTINATION REACHED

Just as the conductor said, you soon feel the train moving faster. You're now in open country with few bridges to cross or bends in the tracks. The train moves faster and faster. It soon reaches 150 miles per hour (241 kph), its maximum speed. Your skin tingles as you watch the scenery rush by. This is what you have been waiting for! As the train draws nearer to Providence, it gradually slows down again. You glide into the station, retrieve your carry-on bag from the bin, and head for the nearest door. The conductor asks if you enjoyed your ride. You tell her yes and that you wish you could stay on all the way to Boston. You liked your high-speed train experience, and you're already looking forward to the return trip.

ON TO BOSTON

When the train arrives back in Boston, it often starts its route again almost immediately. Most Acela Express trains make multiple round trips each day. The expensive machinery must earn its keep. However, it is late in the day, and the train you were on is ending its long workday. While some crew members leave for home, the conductor still has plenty of work left to do. She prepares a report on the day's journeys, noting any accidents, delays, or unscheduled stops and the reasons for them.

CHRISTINE SUCHY

Christine Suchy works at Amtrak, where she helps direct the company's finances. Suchy came to the United States from her native Germany in 1998. In 2006, she went to work for Amtrak. Her first job was negotiating agreements between Amtrak and other railway companies that wanted to use its rails. Now she works to obtain the federal funds that Amtrak needs to expand its high-speed operations. Organizing all the parties involved is hard work, and sometimes Amtrak doesn't receive the grants it needs. However, Suchy never tires of her job. "I love trains," she says.

Though cleaning crews have come on board at various stops along the way to clean up trash, there may be another final cleanup now. Then the train heads back to the rail yard, where the whole process will begin again. It takes a lot of people with different skills to keep a high-speed train running, and we all benefit from their efforts.

Trains are stored at rail yards when they are not in use.

Maglev trains will likely play a key role in the future of high-speed rail travel.

WHAT'S NEXT?

The future of high-speed trains can be summed up in one word—maglev. The few maglevs running today have shown that these trains can far outdo electric trains in speed, efficiency, safety, and environmental impact. The main challenge facing today's engineers and scientists in designing new maglev systems is the great expense. High costs come in part from constant computer monitoring needed to keep the trains "afloat" above the tracks, as well as from the trains' vulnerability to certain weather conditions. However, the great advantages of maglev for future travel on Earth and beyond may make it worth the effort.

UNDERWATER TRAINS

The Chunnel has connected England and the European continent underwater for several decades. But what about a train that could connect New York City to London across more than 3,000 miles (4,828 km) of the Atlantic Ocean? As farfetched as such a project may seem, scientists and engineers believe it is possible. A maglev train traveling in an underwater tunnel at 5,000 miles per hour (8,047 kph) could make the trip in an hour, compared to an eight-hour flight. Engineers believe that if the enclosed tunnel were to float 150 to 300 feet (46 to 91 m) beneath the ocean, it would avoid the tremendous pressure of the ocean floor.

This plan would also allow for flexibility in the tunnel, which would soften the impact of underwater disturbances. Cables would be attached to the tunnel to further increase its stability. Expensive and time-consuming as the construction of this underwater train would be, it would unite the United States and Europe as never before.

IS THE SKY THE LIMIT?

If maglev trains can cross oceans, why can't they visit outer space? The National Aeronautics and Space Administration (NASA) has been working for decades on the possible launching of spacecraft into low Earth orbit using maglev technology. Cargo could be launched on a track built into a mountainside at a height of 20,000 feet (6,096 m). This so-called Startram would launch a "space train" at a speed of 18,000 miles per hour (28,968 kph), fast enough to put it into orbit. Launching people into space would be a bigger challenge. Scientists estimate that the launch track would have to be about 1,000 miles (1,609 km) long and 12 miles (19 km) high. It would cost billions to build, but the payoff might be well worth it. Virgin Galactic, a British airline, is planning to take passengers into space at a cost of $200,000 per person. A maglev StarTram could lower the price to $50,000. For high-speed trains of the future, even the sky may not be the limit. ✷

Virgin Galactic's SpaceShipTwo *craft might one day allow passengers to travel into outer space with the help of maglev technology.*

CAREER STATS

MECHANICAL ENGINEERS

MEDIAN ANNUAL SALARY (2012): $80,580

NUMBER OF JOBS (2012): 258,100

PROJECTED JOB GROWTH (2012–2022): 5%, slower than average

PROJECTED INCREASE IN JOBS (2012–2022): 11,600

REQUIRED EDUCATION: Bachelor's degree

LICENSE/CERTIFICATION: State license

CIVIL ENGINEERS

MEDIAN ANNUAL SALARY (2012): $79,340

NUMBER OF JOBS (2012): 272,900

PROJECTED JOB GROWTH (2012–2022): 20%, faster than average

PROJECTED INCREASE IN JOBS (2012–2022): 53,700

REQUIRED EDUCATION: Bachelor's degree

LICENSE/CERTIFICATION: State license

RAILROAD WORKERS

MEDIAN ANNUAL SALARY (2012): $52,400

NUMBER OF JOBS (2012): 113,800

PROJECTED JOB GROWTH (2012–2022): –3%, a decline

PROJECTED INCREASE IN JOBS (2012–2022): –4,000

REQUIRED EDUCATION: High school diploma or equivalent

LICENSE/CERTIFICATION: Certification varies by position and employer

Figures reported by the United States Bureau of Labor Statistics

RESOURCES

BOOKS

Coiley, John. *Train*. New York: DK Publishing, 2009.

Eason, Sarah. *How Does a High-Speed Train Work?* New York: Gareth Stevens Publishing, 2010.

Mara, Wil. *From Kingfishers to . . . Bullet Trains*. Ann Arbor, MI: Cherry Lake Publishing, 2013.

FACTS FOR NOW

Visit this Scholastic Web site for more information on high-speed trains:
www.factsfornow.scholastic.com
Enter the keywords **High-Speed Trains**

GLOSSARY

amenities (uh-MEN-uh-teez) features of a product or service that provide comfort or pleasure

architect (AHR-ki-tekt) a person who designs buildings and supervises the way they are built

couple (KUHP-uhl) to connect train cars

efficient (i-FISH-uhnt) working very well and not wasting time or energy

friction (FRIK-shuhn) the force that slows down objects when they rub against each other

infrastructure (IN-fruh-struhk-chur) the basic facilities serving an area, such as transportation and communications systems

locomotives (loh-kuh-MOH-tivz) engines used to push or pull railroad cars

pantograph (PAN-tuh-graf) a device that transfers electric current from an overhead wire to a train or other vehicle

piston (PIS-tuhn) a disk or cylinder that moves back and forth in a larger cylinder

right-of-way (RITE-UHV-WAY) the strip of land acquired by a railroad to use for tracks

INDEX

Page numbers in *italics* indicate illustrations.

ABOUT THE AUTHOR

STEVEN OTFINOSKI has written more than 160 books for young readers, including books on cars, airplanes, and trains. He lives in Connecticut.